Lexington

Pictorial Nostalgia

BY

Barton K. Battaile

COMMEMORATING 1775 - 1975 BICENTENIAL

To my mother, Elizabeth de la Fontaine Kinkead Battaile.

CONTENTS

PREFACE

Can you remember when Lexington was larger than Chicago? Believe it or not, it was at one time. However, there is no one alive today that can remember "the old Lexington". In pioneer days, it was quite a prosperous city, but failed to grow rapidly. The population did not reach 50,000 until 1950. Despite Lexington's failure to populate, it continued to occupy a place of some importance in several lines of business and services, and especially in entertainment.

Understanding Lexington's place in pioneer times is not easy, for we must remember that from 1790, when the first United States Census was taken, until 1830, Lexington was Kentucky's largest city. In 1820, Kentucky was the nation's sixth largest state in population; this made Kentucky important in the nation's business and politics.

Back to our comparison of Lexington to Chicago; Chicago had no permanent settlers until the late 1820's. The first map of Chicago was not drafted until 1830, while at the same time Lexington had a population of 6,020. Seven years later, a census was taken of Chicago, revealing 4,170 inhabitants. However, in the 1840's, Chicago rapidly outraced Lexington in population as a result of passable waterways, and the invention of the steamboat.

As Louisville surpassed Lexington, the people realized they were not to be the business center of Kentucky any longer, unless they had something with which to compete. As a result, Lexington became pioneer of the railroad.

By 1850, Lexington ranked only third in Kentucky following Louisville and Covington, which were both located on the Ohio River. At the turn of the century, Lexington dropped fourth, being behind Newport. By 1910, it jumped back up to third and then in 1960, rose to second. However, Lexington remained all this time to be known as the center point of the "Blue Grass Region". It continued a role larger than its population would reveal.

While Lexington was taking a back seat to "Steam Boat Bill", which set Lexington back at least a century, it enlarged its position as an educational and medical center and as an important retail and wholesale city. It became the location of major sales for tobacco and livestock and most important, the center of the world's leading horse breeding country. Comparatively to larger cities, Lexington offered much more than others in horse racing, theater, and entertainment.

During these important days of small population, many outsiders commented that Lexington was the most metropolitan city of its size. Maybe some of this will explain why old timers believe that Lexington was a right lively place to be in the "old days". Also, maybe you can understand why Kentucky's reputation was nationwide more so than her population.

ACKNOWLEDGEMENTS

I wish to thank the following people who have made it possible for me to publish this book.

Mrs. Art Baumohl, for allowing me to copy select pictures from her collection.

Bert Oram, for allowing me to use his book, "Illustrated Lexington", printed in 1919 by Transylvania Printing Company and presented to him while visiting his wife's family off the coast of Germany.

Mr. Fletcher Vick, who presented me with a very old book printed in 1906.

Arthur Lawson, of the Lexington Public Library, for his assistance with research.

Mrs. Mary Powell Phelps, head of the Lexington Public Library, for letting me copy old pictures on file in the Library vault.

My daughter, Matilda Battaile Moore, for her assistance in editing.

My granddaughter, Sarah M. Katzenmaier, for typing the manuscript.

I wish to express my appreciation to the late Charles Staples, author of "History Of Pioneer Lexington", the person most responsible for my renewed interest in Lexington history.

For the cover design by Steve Cornett.

Barton Kinkead Battaile

History

of

Shelby and Clay

ISAAC SHELBY

A book commemorating the bicentennial of Lexington would not be complete without a picture and a brief history of Isaac Shelby, Kentucky's first Governor. There are a number of his descendants still living in and around Lexington.

Isaac Shelby was born December 11, 1750, near the North mountain in Maryland, where his father and grandfather settled after their emigration from Wales. His father, General Evan Shelby, fought in the French and Indian War and distinguished himself in the Revolutionary War.

Isaac had only a plain English education but was born with a strong constitution inherited from his father. He was a very intelligent young man with a great deal of common sense.

He was a lieutenant in his father's company. After his garrison was disbanded in July, 1775, he came to Kentucky as a surveyor with Henderson & Co. Because of impaired health, he returned home after a year.

In the spring of 1779 he was elected a member of the Virginia Legislature but his land was found to be a part of North Carolina. He was appointed a Colonel in the North Carolina militia. He decided in 1780 that he must fight for his country and joined the Army.

The legislature of North Carolina passed a vote of thanks to Colonel Shelby and presented him with a pair of elegant swords for his patriotic conduct in the attack and defeat of the enemy on King's mountain on October 7, 1780. These swords, one with a solid gold handle and the other one with a pearl handle, belonged to this writer along with the engraving from which came the Jouett portrait.

In 1783 Isaac Shelby returned to Boonesborough, Kentucky, where he married Susanna Hart. She was the daughter of Captain Nathaniel Hart, one of the first settlers of Kentucky. Their children were: James Shelby was born in 1784. He married Mary Pindell, daughter of the famous Revolutionary surgeon, Dr. Richard Pindell, of Maryland. Sarah, born 1785, married Dr. Ephraim McDowell of Danville. Evan was born in 1787 and married Nancy Warren. He fought in the War of 1812 and died in Mexico in 1875. Thomas Hart Shelby was born May 27, 1789. He first married Mary McDowell and his second wife was Mary Ann Bullock. He died February 14 ,1869. Susanna, born 1791, was married first to James McDowell. Her second husband was James Shannon who was a minister to Mexico. Her third husband was John Mc-

ISAAC SHELBY

Kinney and her fourth was Dr. John Fishback. Isaac Shelby, Jr. was born in 1795 and died in 1886. Nancy was born 1792 and married the Reverend Sam K. Nelson, founder of Centre College, Danville. John was born in 1797 and died in 1813. Letitia, born 1799, married Colonel Stewart Todd. One child, Katherine, who was born in 1801, died as an infant. Alfred, born 1804, married Virginia Hart, daughter of Nathaniel Hart of Woodford County, Kentucky.

Shelby was a member of the conventions that met in Danville for the purpose of separation of Kentucky from Virginia and was also a member of the convention which formed the first constitution of Kentucky in April, 1792. May, 1792, he was elected Kentucky's first governor. At the expiration of his term he returned to private life but in 1812, he was again elected to the state's highest office.

He was offered the post of Secretary of War by President Monroe in 1817 but because of his advanced age and ill health, he declined. He was attacked with paralysis in 1820 and died July 18, 1826. His mind was clear to the end of his life. He was a member of the Presbyterian Church and erected a house of worship in his own land.

11

Monument to Isaac Shelby, Kentucky's first governor, located one mile South of Junction City outside of Danville, Kentucky. This is where he is buried.

HENRY CLAY

Henry Clay, the son of a clergyman, was born in Hanover County, Virginia, on April 12, 1777. His father died while he was quite young, so consequently his education was acquired at a common school. At an early age he began work in the office of a clerk of the high court of chancery in Richmond, Virginia. He was admitted to the practice of law at the age of 20.

Soon he moved to Lexington, Kentucky, and studied for another year. He joined a debating society and after his embarrassment at his first attempt, he became a polished speaker. His extensive practice proved lucrative because of his genius, legal knowledge and practical accuracy.

Mr. Clay's political career started at this time. His first effort in 1798, gradual freeing of the slaves, met with failure.

In 1803, he was elected a member of the Kentucky legislature and in 1806, he became a United States Senator. After the expiration of his term of office, he was reelected to the legislature and was chosen speaker. Henry Clay went back to the U. S. Senate in 1809, at which time foreign powers were infringing on the neutrality rights of our country. He was instrumental in passing the protective policy of "domestic manufacturers" which we know as the "American System".

In 1814, Mr. Clay was appointed a commissioner to negotiate the Treaty of Ghent. After those negotiations were complete, he and two colleagues went to London for negotiations which led to a commercial convention and from this came most of our commercial arrangements with foreign powers.

In 1824 Mr. Clay was a presidential candidate but the House of Representatives elected John Quincy Adams. As the Whig nominee in 1844, he was defeated by Mr. Polk. He continued to serve in the Senate until his health forced his retirement.

He died June 28, 1852, at the age of 76. His death stopped all business and adjourned the Congress. His funeral was attended by thousands, among them congressmen and mayors of the cities around Washington. His body was returned to Lexington, Kentucky, and his final resting place in the Lexington Cemetery on West Main Street.

Ashland, his home on East Main Street in Lexington, is a national shrine which is visited by thousands each year.

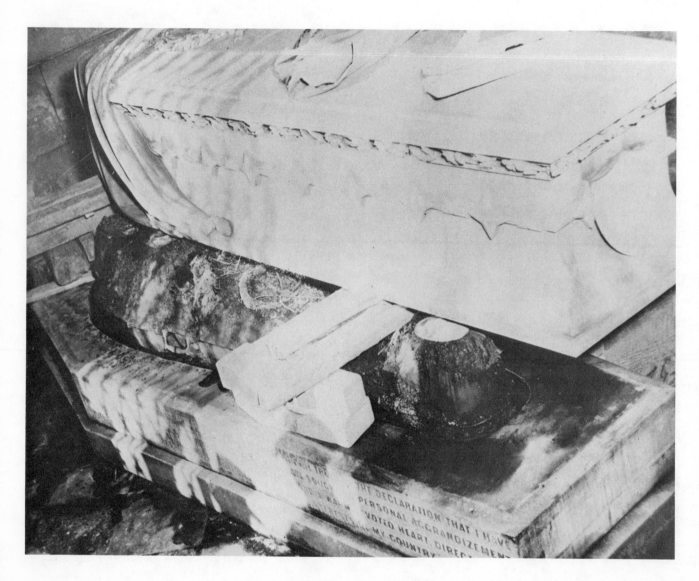

Under Henry Clay's Tomb

Henry Clay's crypt was opened up some years ago to see if any damage had been done to it from leakage over the years. If you will look very closely, you will see a bouquet and in the middle of it a ring.

14

Old Houses

Former residence of M. P. Lancaster, which is located at the corner of Third and Mill Streets, it was for many years owned by Transylvania University and occupied by their presidents. The gentleman at the left is J. Hull Davidson, husband of Lancaster's daughter. Davidson was the manager of the Phoenix Hotel for many years and also served as the Mayor of Lexington.

Formerly used as a Boy's School by Professor Merrick, and later as the I. O. O. F. Temple, this house at 216 North Broadway is now being used by the Women's Club of Central Kentucky.

White Hall, Lexington, Ky. This handsome Southern Home was last used as a residence by Dr. and Mrs. James C. Carrick. It stands at the corner of Third and Limestone Streets. Begun in the early part of the 19th century, White Hall was once owned by Chief Justic Thomas A. Marshall, who sold it in 1857 to Mayor Claudius Johnson, husband of Rosa Vertner, the famous Blue Grass poetess. Gideon Shryock, renowned architect of Morrison College and the old Capitol at Frankfort, designed its graceful columns. It is now owned and occupied by the Whitehall Funeral Chapel, Inc.

Mrs. Leslie Carter, the famous stage actress, born Carolyn Louise Dudley in Lexington on June 10, 1863 in the large two story house pictured above. It stood on West Main under the Viaduct.

Samuel McMeekin, David McMurtry House, SE corner Short and Jefferson Streets, 592 West Short Street. Samuel McMeekin, who in 1843 was operating a machine shop and carding factory on SE corner of Short and Spring Streets, had Robert King build his residence in 1838. Robert King, who was a carpenter and contractor, bought the lot (66′ on Short Street, 110′ on Jefferson) from Samuel Buckner, wife Louisa M. of Bourbon County. King and wife, Angela, conveyed the property to McMeekin on July 17, 1838. McMeekin, now of Hamilton County, Ohio, sold the house to Thomas Hemmingway, his Lexington representative. The house had been sold at Public Auction for Short Street Improvement in August, 1841 to Mayor Daniel Bradford who bought it in for the city at that time. Hemmingway and wife, Jane, sold the property to David McMurtry on March 20, 1854. He conveyed it to his wife, Mary Jane, in 1884. His mother, Mrs. Mary Shields, had also had it conveyed to her on March 27, 1856. McMurtry was the brother of the architect, John McMurtry.

This home which was located on East Main opposite Walnut, owned by R. Leslie Combs, later converted into the Gem Hotel and demolished for the Lafayette Hotel, is presently the site of the Kentucky Central Life Insurance Building.

This old house on Tucker Street was at the rear of the Main Street Baptist Church which faced the Robert S. Todd's home.

Formerly owned by the Dewees family, this house was located on East Short Street. Later it was occupied by the Benjamin Gratz family for many years.

This was the house of Dr. J. S. Wilson, later owned by O. L. Bradley and now occupied by Featherston's Garage.

Former residence of John Gilbert King who managed Nelson's Hemp Factory, this house at 225 South Limestone is now the location of Shug Glenn Buick, a used car lot.

Dr. John W. Peck lived here on the southeast corner of Mill and Maxwell. The Kaiser family formerly lived at this site for many years. After Kaisers death, it was occupied by the Christian Church.

The above residence was owned by Miss Lucky G. Shelby and her brother, Edmond Shelby who are now deceased, both were connected with Johnson School, where she was a teacher and he was the principal. With them lives their nephew Ned Shelby, and after their death, he moved to Florida, where he now resides. The building was later sold and razed, where the Fraternal Order of Police now have their offices and clubroom.

The Dr. William Offutt Home, at North Broadway and New Streets, the proposed site of two town houses, was formerly owned and built by W. H. Loughridge and his wife, Fannie Bruce. The above picture, was taken by Mrs. Loughridge on October 24, 1908 and to the right shows part of the King House.

E. S. Delong residence, located on the southeast corner of Fourth and Limestone Streets is now occupied by the Lexington Junior High School.

Home of Susan Shelby, daughter of Isaac Shelby who was Kentucky's first Governor, this house was located on South Limestone opposite the University of Kentucky. It was later owned by a U. K. Professor Miller and turned into a Fraternity House. It was torn down and the Theological Seminary was built on the property. Interestingly enough, there is a cave under the property, which came out on Rose Street on the property of M. J. Crutcher, who was the superintendent of the buildings at U. K. Later, the cave was sealed off.

This was the location of the Slave Jail on the south side of West Short Street at 510, which is opposite where the Children's Home was later located.

Home of Robert L. Zimmerman, Sr., at his death, this house was left to Robert L. Zimmerman, Jr. He and his mother, Katherine lived there until it was razed in 1973. The house was located at 434 East High Street. It was built for Mr. Zimmerman by a carpenter named Mr. Edward Erd.

The home of Mrs. Bell on East Main, now the Esplanade and later used by Dr. Stockdell, was the initial effort of what later became the Central Christian Church. The building on the left was the O'Day Plumbing Co., which was one of Lexington's leading plumbers.

Saint Peter Catholic Church on North Limestone, was erected in 1837 and demolished in 1939.

Pullams Slave Jail, 149 North Broadway, was demolished in 1901 to make room for The Elks Club. This building was erected by Mathias Shryock, father of Gideon Shryock who was architect of Morrison Chapel and other famous buildings in Central Kentucky. It was used by slavers, Pullman, Blackwell, Murphy and others. Felix Murphy, son-in-law of Blackwell, later moved to Nelson County and became the county Judge in 1864. General O. Q. Howard and staff used this building as headquarters for the Freedoms Bureau and afterwards was used by Dr. J. A. Coyle, Dr. Stucky and other physicians. When this building was destroyed, the cap stone was found cut on the south side of the building. It was removed by Dick Webb and placed on the building on East Main opposite Rose Street, which is now Mammouth's Garage.

This was the old Harrison School, originally located at 618 West Main. Observe the separate doors for male and female. To the right of the school, 620 West Main, is the house originally owned by the Heddington family. At their death, the heirs sold it to Edward Dowling; then by will it was transferred to Margaret Dowling, his daughter. Now it is owned by Mrs. Frank A. Whele, widow of Dr. Frank A. Whele, who lives there presently with her daughter, Jane.

Formerly the home of Vice President Breckenridge and later the home of Mrs. Elizabeth K. Battaile, this house is located at 429 West Second Street. In the above picture, Mrs. E. S. Kinkead is holding the horse and Mrs. Battaile is in the carriage.

The McCulla residence, facing West High Street and the First Methodist Church, was a weatherboarded log cabin, built in 1794. There was a great controversy between the local preservation groups and the Urban Renewal, which continued for quite some time. It was eventually torn down, due to Urban Renewal.

This house was first occupied by the Swift family. Later it was sold to L. B. Todd. Now it is the site of the Calvary Baptist Church at 128 East High, near the Harrison Street Viaduct.

Home of Dr. J. G. Foster, it is located on the corner of Main and Spring Streets.

Joel and Alice Higgin's home, is located at 600 East High, near Lexington Avenue.

This was the home of Robert S. Todd, father of Mary Todd Lincoln. Lincoln stayed here three days en route to serve his term in Congress. This building has caused much controversy concerning making it a State Shrine. It is located at 574 East Main.

This is the home of Dr. Fred Ridgley, located on Market at Second. The building at the back has been torn down for a parking lot.

Anna Morris Boswell, wife of Orville Shelby of Tennessee and mother of General Hoe Shelby of Missouri, later married Benjamin Gratz. Their daughter, Miriam Gratz married Commodore Crosby. Another daughter, Ann Gratz married Thomas H. Clay. Mr. and Mrs. Clay were the parents of Miss Henrietta Clay.

"The Meadows" was the former home of the War-fields, Ashers, Magoffins, and Stolls. The farm has since been subdivided.

Originally D. C. Goodloe's home, this house was later used as the St. Joseph Hospital. At one time it was the KA Fraternity House. It is now the Dagley home, located on Linden Walk.

Last owned by Nettie Arnold, this house on 121 Forest Avenue has recently been torn down.

"Ellerslie", built in the late 1700's by Levi Todd, for which Lake Ellerslie was named. It was located on the Richmond Road, near Todds Road and was for many years a well known fishing club.

This photograph was taken in 1920 at the auction of the household furnishings of the Green Hills Mansion of J. B. Haggin, on the Elmendorf Farm.

This is a slave house next to Wendover Stables on the west side of Limestone Street. Slaves were kept here overnight when being transported.

Formerly the Orphan's Home on West Third Street, this has since been replaced with the Archway leading to Hampton Court.

Paradise Farm, located on Russell Cave Road, formerly owned by Mr. and Mrs. James Headley and at their death, the house was razed and converted for industrial use.

This was one of the first homes in Lexington, owned by the Geohagans.

Charlie McCarthy, one of Lexington's leading attorneys, can be seen sitting on the curb in front of his home with his family in the background. The house was located near the Viaduct on West Main.

The Woosley House was called the Little Inn. It was a rooming house located on East High, where Shug Glenn Buick is now located.

A very early picture of Ashland, home of Henry Clay, is located on US 25 South on the corner of Sycamore and East Main Streets.

St. John's Academy, a parochial school for boys was established in 1854 at the back of St. Peter's Catholic Church on North Limestone. In 1902, it merged with St. Paul's School. This old two story building faced Walnut Street and was torn down in 1909.

Originally the home of Judge J. R. Morton on the east side of Short Street, it then became a parking lot opposite the Esplanade. Then the Greyhound Bus Company used it for a terminal. The property was then purchased by the City of Lexington to erect a jail.

The two houses above were formerly owned by Dr. Dudley. The one on the left was his residence and the little one on the right was used as his office. It is said that he kept his cadavers in the basement. His home was purchased by William Temple Withers, who in October of 1881 entertained King Kalakaua of the Sandwich Islands, the first foreign sovereign to visit Lexington. The Embassy Club, which opened the night prohibition on beer was lifted was the next occupant. When the club closed, it was bought by the Thoroughbred Record, the present owner. The little house now, Rebel's Rest Antique Shop, operated by Mr. and Mrs. Bert Halbert.

This brick house on East Third Street opposite Transylvania was the residence of J. Hull Davis, the manager of the Phoenix Hotel and Mayor of Lexington.

This building on High and Limestone St. was originally an antique shop. Later, it was purchased by Charles Jett, and was an appliance store, a loan company, and now is the Bank of the Bluegrass.

This house on the northeast corner of High and Limestone was the scene of a murder at the turn of the century of a black man, named Shipp, by a white man who had discovered Shipp with his wife.

This was the Jury for the Shipp killing.

Residence of Louis desCognets, Main Street and Forest Avenue.

This was the Molloy
Home on Angliana
Avenue, which later
became a vacant lot
and now is the
Vaughn Tobacco
Redryer.

41

In 1902, this house at 331 North Broadway, was owned by Dr. Archie Coyle. Also living in this house was John W. Eastwood, who was a clerk at Kelly's Fish Company near the corner of Broadway and Short. Presently living there is Mrs. Margaret McElhone, n e e Saunier.

The house shown above, at 335 North Broadway, in 1902 was owned by John Pew, secretary of the Lexington Water Company. The house was bought by Mrs. Lucy S. Collier, Head Mistress of Colliers School for children in need of a more disciplinary atmosphere. She was known for being one of the strictest teachers in Lexington. She was known to have cracked knuckles, thrown books, kicked students, and other unmentionable punishments. To mention a few of her pupils, I can remember these: Frank Vaughn, Lucy Vaughn, Louis Haggin, Jimmy Haggin, Joe Skain, Mary Lydia Cleek, Dorothy Cleek, Barton K. Battaile, Douglas Gay, Dr. Carl Wheeler, Warren L. Bain, Willie C. Coleman, Betty Powell Roades, William Harting, Joseph Harting, Don Hayes Glass, Dr. William K. Massie, Joe Logan, Margaret Massie, Charlotte Bowman, Dr. Woolfork Barrow, Matt Clay, Warfield Gratz, and Peter Powell.

In 1902, this beautiful home at 319 North Broadway was owned by Morrison H. Beard and his wife Molly. In 1928, W. M. Dunn and his wife, Maude bought the house.

The house at 353 S. Mill St. was owned in 1902 by John W. Gunn, who was a civil engineer. The house was also occupied by William and Mary Gunn. In the 1928 directory, Mr. Dunn was listed as the only occupant in the house. He was still living there in 1945. In 1968, the property was owned by Surene Divine. In 1970, Keith Sleter lived there. In 1971, the directory stated that Paul Gutherie lived there.

This is the Steven C. Saunier house, located at 703 West High Street. Mr. Saunier was a blacksmith with his business located at 153-155 Sycamore, later known as Saunier Alley. This house was also occupied by Helen Saunier, bookkeeper for McGovern Brothers, who ran a poultry business on Vine Street. Later, John C. and Joseph A. Saunier lived there, and presently, Mrs. Dorothy Oldfield lives there.

The Hayman house, on the corner of Vine and Spring Streets, was available to the public for weddings.

Old
Buildings

A tintype taken when the Herald Leader Building on the corner of Short and Market, was a furniture store. The building to the left later became the University Book Store, owned by Frank Battaile.

The Fayette National Bank, later the First Security National Bank and Trust Company, and now used for offices, is shown from a view looking east toward Cheapside and Upper Street.

A tintype of Cheapside in the late 1860's, was later the site of the Northern Bank Building.

This monument to William T. Berry was on the corner of Upper and Main Streets in the courthouse yard. During the construction of the present courthouse, this monument disappeared and was never found.

Originally the Stage Depot, then the Windover Stables, located on the west side of Limestone, north of Lyon Firehouse.

View of the old courthouse from Main looking to Cheapside, with Short Street on the right, this barber pole is where the First National Bank Building was built. This building burned May 27, 1897.

One of Henry Clay's law offices, also the offices of G. B. Kinkead, General Houston and other lawyers, located to the west of the Fire Department on Short Street.

Old Mule (Street Car) stables on south side of west Vine Street with Spring Street to right of photo.

Melodeon Hall was one of the first theaters in Lexington, located on the second floor of the southwest corner of Main and Upper Streets, with a seating capacity of 300. Since 1817, there has been a drug store on the ground floor.

In this closeup of the Melodeon Theater, you can see the original wallpaper still hanging.

During the construction of the courthouse which burned May, 1897, this was used for the county clerk office on Upper Street. From left to right are William Bush, Gip Simmons, William Dishman, Jessie Hall, Col. J. R. Graves, Estes Garrett, Waller Bullock, and J. R. Jewell.

Last chair taken out of the Melodeon Hall Theater.

The first lawsuit set for trial in the 1900 courthouse was the Phoenix National Bank, et al vs Northwestern Life Insurance vs policy held by J. R. Jewell during February of 1900. Dr. Kinnaird is on the witness stand.

The South half of the Blanton building (cont'd next page) with railing removed. The gentleman in front is Gary Jarbut, possessor of many pictures secured for this book, that was taken from the saloon walls. The building was de-molished in 1950.

M. Giron's Confectionery. The building as it was originally built in the early part of the 19th century, was forty four feet wide and fifty feet long. In 1915 the south half of the structure was demolished, reducing the width to twenty two feet, the present width is unaltered. The building is wood structure and brick bearing walls construction. The second floor has molding of the Greek Revival period, with only the Cherry folding doors separating two upper rooms missing. The front of the building has Tuscan columns on the first and second level, the columns still remaining on the second level facade, where was a confectionery, owned by Monsieur Giron, on the ground level in which a Swiss cook, M. Ritter, created pastries, pies and mammoth (cattelated) cake which Lexington citizenry presented to Marquis de Lafayette, when he visited Lexington in the 1825 period. The second level contains two grand ball rooms, in which dances of great splendor were held. Mary Todd Lincoln was a frequent visitor of the ball rooms, and spent many evenings dancing among the Lexington aristocracy. After M. Giron left Lexington the structure became a saloon and grocery store; the second level became a dancing studio of a well known Frenchman. Since that time the building use has changed frequently. The present use is that of commercial. The present owner of the building is Mr. Richard Blanton of Blanton Realty Agency, occupying the second floor. The first floor tenant is Postal Finance Company.

The M. P. Lancaster Store, later occupied by B. B. Smith and Company, was located on the south side of Main Street, just east of Mill.

Inside view of the Main Street Christian Church, later site of the Union Depot and now occupied by a department store, parking lot and offices.

This view showing Main Street east from Mill Street in 1894. You will notice that the Fayette Bank Building had not been erected at this time.

This was the scene of a Baptism at the Pleasant Green Baptist Church in 1898. The old City Jail in the background was between Upper and Broadway at the South end of Mill Street. Ligget and Myers is now located at this site.

After a fire at the First Baptist Church, this picture was taken on February 3, 1867.

I hereby authorize Thomas J Hood to sell for cash at the best price he can obtain at private sale, a negro man called Charles Mailor belonging to the estate of William J Carter decd. — Said negro man is now in the county of Carter, of a yellow complexion and about 45 years old. I further hereby ratify and confirm all the acts and deeds of my said Attorney herein authorized.

Given under my hand and seal in the City of Lexington this 26th of March 1850

Isaac Shelby (Seal)
Adm of
Wm J Carter decd

This picture was taken from a tintype of 1885. You can see the City National Bank, Berkley and Murphy Offices on the second floor, and the Union and Harrison House to the left of the bank, Apostolic Times News and Job Printing Office.

This picture of King Solomon was taken from a portrait by S. S. Price.

This site is the grave of William "King" Solomon, hero of the cholera epidemic. He dug graves for the victims after being sold as a slave. Solomon, who died in 1854 at the age of 79, was buried near the entrance of the Lexington Cemetery. His casket, which was considered the finest in Lexington, was furnished by the community.

Formerly the Opera House, before it moved its location to North Broadway, this was the Brower Building after being decorated for July 4. Parades were held on July 4th with elaborate decorations all up and down Main Street.

Taken on Water Street in 1918, this was Ike Shelby, the great, great, great grandson of Isaac Shelby, Kentucky's first Governor.

The Main Street Christian Church, after its purchase by contractors in 1892, was the scene of the Rice-Campbell Debate, in 1843. Henry Clay was the moderator.

Erected in 1850, by Professor Beverly Hicks for a Boys' School, he then used it for his residence when he retired. It was located on the northeast side of Main Street between Walnut and Deweese Streets, and later housed the O'Day Plumbing Company. It was also used for many years as a slave jail by visiting dealers, and is now the site of business buildings.

Wilson and Starks Clothing and Tailoring Store was located on Main Street. Pictured above are Warren Frazier, Tipton Miller, C. M. Alquist, William Thompson, Ole Pearson, Charles Nass, Steve McCulla, Malachi Sheen, W. M. Milton, E. P. Perry, Ed Wickliffe, and Emil Schaeffer, in 1890.

Christ Church, the first Episcopal church west of the Allegheny Mountains was established in 1796, four years after Kentucky became a state. On May 5, 1974, this church had the honor of housing the Princess Margaret and Lord Snowden of Great Britain for Sunday worship service.

The old Police Station, located on Water Street, is shown behind Estes, Garrett, and Ellis. Estes was the grandfather of Lee Allen Estes who was with the State Police for many years. He did a magic show for safety.

Lyons Firehouse was at 147 South Limestone where Peter Vinegar preached "Watch That Snake", "Hell's One Half Mile From Lexington", and "It's A Damn Hot Day". His most famous saying was, "Do as I say and not as I do".

This picture was taken during the construction of the Union Station on East Main at Harrison Avenue Viaduct.

This old colored Methodist Church on Vine Street extending along the south side of the C. and O. Railroad tracks, just east of Ayres Alley, was later occupied by the rear of Bryan-Hunt Wholesale Grocery. It was erected in 1850 and eventually used by the C. and O. Railroad as an oil house.

To the right, you can see the wooden structure which became the Fayette Bank Building. This was during the streetcar strike of 1913, in May.

Horse drawn wagons carting tobacco on sticks can be seen on South Broadway just below the railroad tracks. At the left, you can see Adams Restaurant, later owned by Johnny Ennis.

The first building east of the McClelland Building was used for offices by M. C. Johnson, General Huston, et. al. It was erected by General Leslie Combs.

The Security Trust Safety Vault Company was located on the corner of Short and Mill. At this time, W. R. Milward Mortuary was located next door to the vault. Across the street, were W. J. Loughridge's office, who was the largest hemp dealer in Fayette County.

On the northwest corner of Short and Market Streets was the Northern Bank Building. On the left was a drugstore owned by Overstreet.

The five story building was McAdams and Morford, a wholesale druggists. It was located on South Water Street, between Vine and Mill Streets. The smaller building on the left was the old Police Station.

Shown is the interior of Smith Watkins Co. Left to Right, Felix Kennedy, James Gardner and J. Rice Walker.

The man to the far right is Mr. Bain, next to him is Mr. James Gardner. This was inside the Van Deren Hardware Company, at 340 West Main.

On the northwest corner of Main and Lime was the California Fruit Store. This was taken during the streetcar strike in May of 1913. Suits could be bought for $15.00 a piece across the street.

The Piggly Wiggly Market stood on the northwest corner of Broadway and Short Streets, and was later taken over by Kroger. Now, a laundromat has moved in. Next door, was the Ellis Drugstore.

The East Tennessee Brewing Company was located at West Third and Hickory Streets. They operated from this location from 1905 to 1910. The beer, called Shamrock, was brewed in Knoxville, Tenn., shipped in kegs and white bottles packed in tin cases. This location is now occupied by Bennie Robinson, Inc. who also distribute malt beverages. In front of this location is where the trolley came down Hickory Street, turned around in front of the Third Street entrance to the Lexington Cemetery. Claude Glass would reverse the trolley line for the conductor who would pay him 5¢ for his services. He would immediately run into the East Tennessee Brewing Company and buy a glass of beer.

THERE IS NOTHING BETTER THAN

SHAMROCK BEER

PRODUCT OF THE

East Tennessee Brewing Co.

SOLD AT ALL LEADING BARS AND CAFES

On yesterday Judge W. B. Kinkead was presented with one of the handsomest canes ever seen in Lexington, by Mr. W. C. Shryock. The cane is made of wood and material from the old court-house, and is as long as the Judge is tall. The main body of the cane is black locust, taken from the window frame in which it is said Henry Clay leaned as he made his famous speech. It is inlaid the full length with sugar-tree, oak, ash and cedar, all taken from various woods in the building. The handle is of black walnut, and the head of ash, inlaid with ash, sugar tree, poplar, sycamore and cherry. In the center of the head is a round piece of brick from the old office of the County Judge. This is encircled with a silver ring taken from the tip of the lightning rod, and another of stone, taken from the steps. The ferule is of copper from the Liberty cap, and the point of steele from the lightning rod. This magnificent cane is really a work of art, which is rendered more valuable because of its composition. The cane will be used by the Judge, and preserved by his sons and grandsons as a relic of the old court-house and the early days of our city and county.

March 21, 1860.   M. L. PIERSON.

PHŒNIX HOTEL,

(Corner of Main and Mulberry Streets,)

Lexington, Kentucky.

THE subscriber begs leave to inform his friends and the public generally, that he has leased this old and well known Hotel, in the city of Lexington, and that he has taken charge of the same.

The House has recently undergone a thorough renovation; the rooms are newly and neatly furnished; and still further improvements will be made to render it in all respects worthy of public patronage, and an agreeable home to those who may avail themselves of its privileges.

Intending to devote his own time and attention to the business, and to surround himself with competent assistants, together with faithful, polite and attentive servants, he gives the assurance to the public that no efforts on his part shall be wanting to make the old Phœnix in all respects worthy of its reputation in its palmiest days.

Professions, however, are too easily and too frequently made to be of much value unless accompanied by corresponding acts, and he, therefore, only asks that the public may test the sincerity of his pledges by giving him a call. They will always find him ready to minister to their comfort in the best manner in his power.

C. T. WORLEY.

Lexington, Jan. 10, 1862—w&twlm.

☞ Frankfort Commonwealth copy to amount $5, and charge Lex. Observer and Reporter.

From the Tri-Weekly Commonwealth of Frankfort, Kentucky, on June 18, 1862, you can see where C. T. Worley is taking over the management of the Phoenix Hotel at the corner of Main and Mulberry Streets and renovation is taking place.

69

History

of

Charles Riley Grannan

CHARLES RILEY GRANNAN

Charles Riley Grannan was born in Paris, Kentucky, around 1870. He made a name and fortune on the race track and gained a national reputation as "a dead game sport". He was married briefly to a New York actress but this marriage was soon forgotten. This man traveled America and Europe following the horses. He built up a fortune of $250,000. in gold convertible currency, which would be about $1,000,000. at the present rate of today.

Grannan returned to Kentucky in approximately 1894, and established the Navarre Cafe* in Lexington in a two story brick building west of Walnut. It was an elaborate affair which was reached by the bridge over Main Street which had been erected for the Main Street Christian Church, site of the exposition which led to the bar, that housed an extensive art exhibit.

He died at 38 in Rawhide, Nevada around 1908. His body was hauled by an express wagon to the saloon for the funeral and later transported to the railroad siding for shipment to Paris, Ky., for interment.

His eulogy was read by a scholarly minister who had been too liberal for his church. After being acquitted of a charge of heresy, he quit the church. The eulogy follows:

"Riley Grannan was born in Paris, Ky., about 40 years ago. I am told that from the position of bellboy in a (Louisville) hotel he arose rapidly to be a celebrity of nationwide fame. He was one of the greatest plungers, probably, this continent has ever produced. He was born in the sunny southland where the brooks and rivers run musically through the luxuriant land; where the magnolia grandiflora, like white stars, glow in a firmament of green. Where crystal lakes dot the greensward and the softened summer breezes dimple the wavelips into kisses for the lilies on the shore; where the air is resonant with the warbled melody of a thousand sweet-voiced birds and redolent with the perfume of many flowers." "He died in Rawhide

---

*Reason for naming Navarre Cafe, Pittsburgh Phil and Ronnie Grannan had a bet going that Henry of Navarre would beat Domino. The horses ran a dead heat, but the odds gave Grannan several thousand dollars. His judgement was vindicated later when Navarre beat Domino three times.

where in winter the shoulders of the mountains are wrapped in garments of ice and, in summer, the blistering rays of the sun beat down upon the skeleton ribs of the desert." The speaker said Grannan "seemed to accept both defeat and victory with equanamity" and "was a man whose exterior was as placid and gentle as any I have seen and an individual absolutely invincible in Spirit. "If you will allow me, I will use a phrase most of you are acquainted with — he was a dead game sport and I say it not irreverently, but fill the phrase as full of practical human philosophy as it will hold and I believe that when you can say one is a "dead game sport" you have reached the climax of human philosophy. I know that there are those who will condemn him. There are those who will believe today he is reaping the reward of a misspent life . . . To those I have no word to say in regard to him. They are ruled by the skeleton hand of the past and fail to see the moral beauty of the type that reached its greatest manifestation in ceremonial piety but of the type that finds expression in a handclasp; the type that finds expression in a word of cheer to a discouraged brother; the type that finds expression in a quiet deed of charity; the type that finds expression in friendship — the sweetest flower that blooms along the dusty highway of life — the type that finds expression in manhood."

"He lived in the world of sport; he wasted his money — so the world says. Did you ever stop to think how God does not put all His sunbeams into corn, potatoes and flour? Did you ever notice the prodigality with which he scatters those beams over the universe? Let these flowers, Riley, with their petaled lips and perfumed breath speak in beauty and fragrance the sentiments that are too tender for words — Goodbye."

The shorthand taking California reporter wrote: "there was not a dry eye in the house."

It is said that one day he was very low in funds and a man staked him to $20,000. Later, he met this man on the street and paid him back. He was no piker.

Above, a portrait of Grannan in his prime.

Daisy Dixon,
Riley Grannan's actress/wife.

This is the house that Riley Grannan bought for his sister in Paris, Kentucky. She was a hundred years old in 1974. Now residing in a nursing home. The house is endowed to the catholic church seen on the left.

These musicians played in the pit at the Lexington Opera House when Lexington was one of the best one night show towns in America. Some of the world's best actors and actresses "trod the boards" and appeared in dramas, musicals, and operettas long to be remembered. This group included, left to right, front rows, Pat Humphreys, John Buchignani, Alfred Wyman, Fred Bagshaw, Harry Wyman, Alfred Wyman; second row, Charles S. Wright, Ellis O. Kidd, Gordon Hunt, Tony Pizassi, Albert McMichael, and Bert Wilson.

Pictures

from

Lexington, Kentucky

1906

The Inter=Urban Electric System

GREAT system of urban electric railways, with Lexington as its centre, is now in course of rapid development, and already brings many miles of splendid territory and many thousands of excellent population practically to our city's doors. Three lines have already been completed—one to Paris, one to Georgetown, and one to Versailles—and hourly service, equal to any given by the best traction lines in the country, now connects those prosperous towns and their rich territory with the Blue Grass Capital.

Numerous other lines are certainties of the near future, and within a short time the inter-urban system will be serving a territory surrounding Lexington which has a population of some two hundred thousand of the best people, and running through the richest agricultural and stock-raising sections, to some of the best and most prosperous cities, towns and villages of the country.

Nothing has been left undone to make the country service ideal, and the wonderful influence this service has exerted on the development of Lexington is manifest to every observer.

SOME STREET RAILWAY HISTORY

Street railway service in Lexington dates from 1887, when the original system was laid out by Mr. A. I. Totten, civil engineer. Few changes have been made in the original lines, except to extend them as the growth of the city made such extension necessary. The city railways and the inter-urban lines are now consolidated into one great system, and together they give a service not excelled anywhere in the South, and equalled in but few places.

FINANCIAL LEXINGTON

The Financial Solidity of the City as Demonstrated by the Record of Her Strong and Reliable Banks and Trust Companies

A Proof of the Desirability of Lexington as a Place for Investment or Residence

THE financial history of Lexington is one that may be studied with profit. The capital surplus and deposits of the eight banks constituting her world of finance, aggregate an amount far greater than usual in a city of like size and population, and the showing made in the semi-annual and quarterly statements issued entitles her to rank among the best banking towns of the country.

In 1875 and 1893, when banks in almost every city, town and hamlet of the land were toppling, and causing ruin to thousands of depositors and stockholders in the crash, the banks of this city stood like so many fortresses—strong and immovable—The interest of both individuals and community safeguarded by the conservative and safe methods employed by the capable and careful men who manage and direct these institutions.

The local money supply made accessible within the past few years by the enterprise and harmony of the Lexington banks has facilitated business transaction in a manner that has contributed immeasurably to the success of this market. There may have been obstacles and drawbacks which hard-working and conscientious merchants or operators failed to surmount or overcome, but for thirty years there has not been a failure of any particular consequence that was traceable to a Lexington bank.

There has been no mushroom growth in the banking business of this city. What has been accomplished is the result of careful planning and thorough execution on the part of able financiers, who have presided over the affairs of Lexington banks. There have been no "wildcat" schemes, no attempt to defraud their depositors, no advantage taken of their creditors, and no desire to shun their obligations, such as have marked similar institutions in some cities of the United States. The result is that the confidence of the public in the banks of Lexington, in their uprightness, in their honesty of purpose and rectitude of conduct, is so deep rooted that it has long since come to be regarded as one of their most valuable assets.

The banks of Lexington are amply equipped to handle the largest lines of business, and are ready and able to extend to all desirable customers the very best accommodations.

LEXINGTON PUBLIC LIBRARY

Taken in 1906, this is a picture of Harrison School on Bruce Street.

83

Agents for the Arms & Burton Horse Cars. The finest and best equipped Stable in the world. Livery of all kinds; Fine Horses on hand for sale; Single Horses, Pairs and Saddle Horses. We also run two Private Horse Cars by Express between Lexington, New York and Boston, for the transportation of Fine Horses.

GARRET D. WILSON,
120 EAST MAIN STREET, LEXINGTON. KENTUCKY.

Z. T. SMILEY,

327-329-331 WEST SHORT ST.,
LEXINGTON, KY.

FIRST CLASS LIVERY.   SPECIAL CAB SERVICE.
EVERYTHING UP-TO-DATE AND FIRST CLASS IN EVERY RESPECT.

Phone 158.

Special Sales of all Kinds of Stock Conducted on the 2nd Monday of Every Month the Year Round.

FINE HORSES ON HAND FOR PRIVATE SALES AT ALL TIMES.

This picture is one of the first ones made of the Scott Hotel after it was built by John Scott and his two sisters in 1902. It was located at 700 South Broadway and had an annex by the Southern Railway tracks. The watchman's house can be seen at the right of the picture. As the hotel business grew, the Scott's built an annex on the SW corner of Anglin and South Broadway and the word "Annex" may be seen in the foyer as you enter the bar that now stands on this spot. The Scotts sold the hotel to Martin and Gus Concannon, their nephews. Gus died in 1957 and Martin in 1973. The Rosenberg brothers bought the Scott Hotel from the Concannons and the bar features live music and go-go girls nightly. It is managed by Fletcher and Barbara Vick.

BLUE GRASS COMMISSION COMPANY
INCORPOPATED.
ROSE STREET and **C & O RAILSOAD**, Lexington, Ky

W. B. TALBERT, Manager.

MANUFACTURERS OF

BLUE GRASS CORN, MEAL and COW FEED.   "PREMIUM" Chicken Feed   "MONARCH" Horse Feed.

RECEIVERS AND SHIPPERS OF

GRAIN, HAY, FEED AND SEED.

The Elevator Shown in the Above Picture is to be Erected in the Near Future.

Pictures

from

"Illustrated Lexington"

1919

ILLUSTRATED LEXINGTON KENTUCKY
"THE HEART OF THE BLUE GRASS"

Illustrated Lexington
Kentucky

**Pictorially Showing the City's Points of Interest.
Public Buildings, Leading Business Houses,
Industrial Interests and Picturesque Scenes**

Lexington

LEXINGTON, KENTUCKY — "The Heart of the Blue Grass."

Where in all this wide world is the famous Blue Grass region of Kentucky unknown? And who, in the remotest parts of the earth, does not associate Lexington, the metropolis of this beuatiful, fertile garden spot of Creation, with the fame and tradition of the Blue Grass?

So well known are the fine thoroughbreds, fleet trotters and fancy saddle horses bred on the great stock farms that surround Lexington, so well advertised is the fine burley tobacco that grows in this favored section, so noted are the colleges that have made Lexington an educational center for more than a century, that little has been said and less is known of the industrial side of Lexington's growth.

Without detracting from the well-known fame of Lexington for horses and tobacco, industry is portrayed pictorially in this souvenir book to a greater extent probably than has ever been attempted in any previous publication. Building construction, flour making and tobacco manufacturing compose the leading industries among more than one hundred manufacturers of various commodities. The exceptional transportation facilities and natural advantages of this commercial center have been responsible for a steady, substantial growth in manufacturing during recent years, and the future presents a rosy outlook for marked industrial expansion in this thriving hub of rich Central Kentucky.

The following facts about Lexington, compiled specially for this book, give full and authentic information about the city of Lexington and the wonderful region surrounding it:

Population, 46,000.

Altitude, 954 feet.

Thirty-four churches.

Three high schools (two white and one colored), 13 public schools and two parochial.

Ten colleges, including University of Kentucky, Transylvania, Hamilton and Sayre Colleges. Annual enrollment of 3,000 students from Kentucky and elsewhere.

Model community school, with outdoor classes, vocational courses, gymnasium, swimming pool and other educational and development facilities.

Lexington College of Music, an institution for art, vocal and instrumental training. Housed in three beautiful buildings and the center of musical culture for the entire Blue Grass Region.

Two fine hospitals, also tuberculosis sanitarium and Eastern State Hospital for Insane.

Commission Form of Government, with five departments, over which Mayor exercises supervisory control.

Handsome public library building. Free circulation of 59,438 books during 1918.

Electric light and power, cheap coal and natural gas, piped from the Eastern Kentucky fields, for all purposes. Light and power furnished to surrounding communities.

Five modern fireproof office buildings from eight to fifteen stories. Daily observations made by U. S. Weather Bureau from highest building.

Assessed valuation: Realty, $24,317,600; personalty, $8,814,965.

Fire equipment: Three triple combination motor engines, one two-way combination motor engine, one gas electric aerial truck, one motor car for chief, three horse-drawn combination chemical, two horse-drawn hose and lineman's wagons, 12,000 feet of two and one-half inch hose, 1,100 feet of chemical hose, six stations, fifty men.

Park and playgrounds: Four parks for white, two for colored, three of which are equipped for playgrounds. Band concerts furnished by city during summer. Two athletic fields and a summer amusement park, with dance hall, amusement concessions, boating and swimming facilities.

Postoffice receipts for 1918: Postage, $212,-580.49; War Savings Stamps, $521,357.19; war revenue stamps, $1,495.03; money orders issued, $281,912.21; cashed, $403,356.77; money order receipts from sub-offices, $619,722.62. Head office and distributing center for 58 other postoffices in Kentucky.

Temperature: Ideal climate. U. S. Weather Bureau report: Annual normal temperature, 55 degrees. Monthly normals: January, 33; February, 36; March, 43; April, 54; May, 64; June, 73; July, 77; August, 75; September, 68; October, 56; November 45 December, 36 degrees.

Precipitation: Well distributed. U. S. Weather Bureau report: Annual normal precipitation, 42.08 inches. Monthly normals: January, 3.83; February, 3.23; March, 4.72; April, 3.34; May, 3.52; June, 3.99; July, 4.44; August, 3.57; September, 2.42; October, 2.22; November, 3.48; December, 3.32 inches.

Fifty-five miles of improved streets, 27 of which are paved; wide streets, paved with wood blocks in business section and asphalt in residential districts; extensive modern white-way lighting system; three reinforced concrete viaducts, total length 2,710 feet; 58.6 miles of sanitary and storm sewers, and a $211,000 sewage disposal plant.

Water system: Investment of $1,500,000; four large reservoirs, covering 410 acres, with capacity of one and one-third billion (1,340,000,000) gallons per day. Pure water, gravity filtered and chlorinated, average hardness, 6.5 grains per gallon. Eighty-seven miles of water mains and 661 fire hydrants. Total pumping capacity of water plant, 12,000,000 gallons per day; average consumption, 3,200,000 gallons per day; 50 cents minimum monthly rate (lowest in United States, fixtures not considered); 42 per cent of all consumers pay minimum bill.

Two daily newspapers, both Associated Press subscribers, with private wires and circulating throughout Kentucky. Both newspapers occupy new, fully equipped, fireproof buildings.

Y. M. C. A., costing, with equipment, $150,-000. Complete, general and physical departments and 55 bedrooms.

Y. W. C. A., centrally located, with all departments and cafeteria. Additional buildings under construction.

Single telephone system, home ownership, with low rates and all long distance connections.

Board of Commerce, Rotary Club and other organizations active in civic development.

Eight banks, with average monthly clearings to September 1 of $3,525,745 (last clearing house report). Deposits, $13,500,000, and resources $25,659,921.87 at the close of business December 31, 1918, an approximate gain of $1,500,000 in deposits and $4,000,000 in resources during 1918, a year of heavy withdrawals for war purposes. First month of 1919 shows increase of 200 per cent in bank clearings, a remarkable record.

Oratorio Society, composed of several hundred singers of Lexington and the Blue Grass, together with 30-piece concert orchestra.

Associated Charities, a federation of social welfare agencies employing trained experts and supported by large individual subscriptions.

Lexington — center of the famous "Blue Grass Region of Kentucky," metropolis of Central Kentucky and county seat of Fayette county — is located on a broad plateau, in the greatest farming and pure-bred stock section in the United States. A slight undulation furnishes natural drainage.

The hub of a great system of railroads, inter-urbans and highways. Five trunk-line railroads, with 44 passenger trains daily; five interurban lines, tapping every section of Central Kentucky, and a network of fine highways make Lexington a trading center for 500,000 within a radius of 50 miles.

A mecca for thousands of tourists the year round. Located on the Dixie Highway, Jackson Highway and National Midland Trail trans-continental routes, and the Boone Way. Fayette county has more than 375 miles of asphalt and macadam roads.

A rapidly growing tobacco manufacturing center. Natural facilities for manufacturing, assembling and distributing are responsible for the location of many industries of varied nature in Lexington.

Greatest loose leaf tobacco market and burley producing section in the world; 14 sales warehouses, with total capacity for handling 10,000,-000 pounds per week. Sales for 1918-19 season, $22,000,000.

Center of the greatest horse breeding country in the world, the most noted stock raising region in the country and the greatest producing center of saddle and fancy horses in the world.

Lexington has the finest trotting track in the world and offers the largest purses. Two running meets are held each year, in addition to the world famous annual trots. The two tracks net an income to Lexington of $2,000,000 yearly.

Center of Eastern Kentucky oil development, with a production for the present year of approximately $20,000,000. Headquarters for operating companies and Kentucky Oil Men's Association.

Headquarters for Eastern Kentucky coal producers. Outlet for fields that produced 30,000,-000 tons mined in 1918, an increase of 10 per cent over previous year.

Greatest bluegrass seed market in the world and one of the five great hemp producing sections of the country.

Distributing center for large wholesale trade over Central, Eastern and Southern Kentucky, Tennessee and West Virginia. Annual income from this source $15,000,000, in addition to $8,000,000 brokerage trade. Wholesale products are dry goods, shoes, hats, caps, gloves, groceries, milling products, drugs, meats, feed, produce, ice, cigars, automobiles, agricultural implements, baking products, lumber, cement, coal, hemp, tobacco, coffee, dairy products, candies, fruit, ice cream, harness, hides, mantels, paper, woodenware, monuments, tents and awnings.

Automobile trade center; 34 automobile and accessory dealers, realizing an annual income of more than $1,000,000.

Finest fair grounds of any city of its size in the United States. The Blue Grass Fair, an annual event, attracts thousands of outside visitors.

Noted as a convention city. Metropolitan hotel facilities and central location of city make Lexington popular for National and State conventions.

Amusements: Opera house, booking best legitimate attractions; Auditorium, seating 2,500; vaudeville house and three high-class movie theatres, with large seating capacity. Plans projected for $500,000 municipal-auditorium building.

The home of Henry Clay, one of many historic points that attract thousands of tourists to Lexington.

A city of beautiful homes, comprising stately Southern mansions of ante-bellum days and the most costly modern structures.

Officers Board of Commerce

J. R. Downing
President

S. T. Harbison
Vice-President

C. F. Dunn
Secretary

Fred G. Stilz
Treasurer

Board of Commerce Officers and Directors: L to R: Samuel B. Walton, Joseph LeCompte, Vice President Shelby T. Harbison, J. Bruce Davis, S. B. Featherson, Treasurer Fred G. Stilz, W. R. Milward, President John R. Downing, Secretary-Manager C. F. Dunn, Professor J. J. Hooper, John G. Cramer, James H. Combs, John J. Hutchinson and Calvert T. Roszell.

Board of Commerce Headquarters at 108 N. Upper Street

Main Street looking East.

The Most Orderly of Disorderly Houses goes up in flames. Some months later Buddy Thompson of Riley & Thompson sold everything including the bricks at Auction.

Main pumping station of the Lexington Water Works.

Spengler's Art and Gift Shop

Interior of Art Department

96

Entrance and Lobby of Ben Ali Theatre.   Finest Moving Picture Theatre in the South.

Stage Showing Screen of Ben Ali Theatre.   Seating Capacity of House, 1,500. Highest Class Orchestra and Best Pictures.

Home of C. F. Brower & Co., Main Street at Broadway
"A Store of Dependable Home Furnishings"

Showing part of Floor Covering Department of C. F. Bower & Co.
"A Store of Dependable Home Furnishings"

Odd Fellows' Orphans' Home.   Located at the end of West 6th Street.

Young Men's Christian Association Building

Lexington Fire Department located on West Short.

Residence of Ollie Honaker

Residence of E. R. Ackerman

Residence of John G. Cramer

Residence of John G. Stoll

Business property owned by E. B. Ellis next to Lexington Leader.

Sale on Loose Leaf Tobacco Market

Lexington Leader Building

THE LEXINGTON LEADER

The Lexington Leader is published week-day afternoons and Sunday mornings by Lexington Leader Company, Incorporated.

The Leader was founded May 1, 1888, and has enjoyed unusual prosperity from the beginning. It has a circulation within the city limits which takes it into practically every substantial home and in the adjoining towns and counties, and along the rural routes it is rapidly becoming as generally read as it is in the city of Lexington.

The Leader occupies a handsome new building on the corner of Short and Market Streets, at the head of historic "Cheapside," which gives it a commanding location. The company has recently installed two additional typesetting machines and a high-speed quadruple press of the latest pattern.

Visitors to the Bluegrass who are interested in artistic interiors and modern publishing equipment are cordially invited to call and see The Leader plant.

Lexington Herald, the only morning newspaper thoroughly covering the Bluegrass region of Kentucky.

Kentucky Traction & Terminal Company — Interurban Car.

Kentucky Trotting Horse Breeders Association Track

Good Samaritan Hospital, Lexington, Ky.
Photo by Thos. A. Knight

MARY A. OTT MEMORIAL BLDG.,
GOOD SAMARITAN HOSPITAL,
LEXINGTON, KY. —27

106

Phoenix and Third National Bank. Capital Stock $800,000, Surplus $110,000. Deposits Five and One-Half Million. W. A. McDowell, President; H. P. Headley, Vice-President; J. R. Downing, Vice-President and Cashier; B. M. Darnaby, Asst. Cashier; C. Y. Freeman, Asst. Cashier.

Main Lobby

Interior View of Directors Room

First and City National Bank
Capital Stock $800,000.00; Surplus $500,000.00; Deposits $5,500,000.00

Presidents Office

Vice President and Cashiers Office

Main Lobby

Bookkeeping Department

View of Work Room, Bank of Commerce. I. W. Mantle, Vice President; O. D. Randolph, Vice President; F. G. Stilz, Cashier; H. A. Stilz, Assistant Cashier. Seven years in business with deposits of over $2,000,000.

Exterior view of Banking House. A few of our patrons.

THE CAMPBELL HAGERMAN COLLEGE
431 W. 2nd St.

Equipped Gymnasium; Tennis, Basket Ball, Golf; Beautiful Grounds; Sites Un-Suite, Heated with Steam, Lighted with Electricity; Hot and Cold Baths; Art Studio, Extensive Library, Chemical and Physical Laboratories; Splendidly Equipped Gymnasium; Tennis, Basket Ball, Golf; Beautiful Grounds; Sites Un-rivalled, on one of the most Beautiful Residence Streets in the very heart of Lexington, the Capital of the Blue Grass Region of Kentucky, a City of Churches and Colleges.

Has six Departments of Instructions — Literature and Science, Music, Art, Elocution, Physical Culture, Domestic Science. Confers A.B. and B.L. Degrees. Prepares for Advanced University Work. Diploma Admits to Eastern Colleges.

B. C. Hagerman, President, Lexington, Ky.

Top: The old Phoenix Hotel — 1825.
Large: Phoenix Hotel — 1920.
Right top insert: Managing director, John Skain.

Present new addition of the Phoenix Hotel.

The New Phoenix Hotel Cafeteria

The Phoenix Hotel prior to erection of new addition in 1911.

Title Guarantee and Trust Co., corner Short and Upper Streets. Member of Federal Reserve System.

Directors Title Guarantee and Trust Co.

Lobby Title Guarantee and Trust Co.

CHAS. A. BAKER,
UNDERTAKER
Morgue, Chapel,
Motor Equipment
Fred R. Baker, Assistant
259 E. Main St., Phone 1522

JOHN MILWARD CO.
Incorporated
FUNERAL DIRECTORS
505-535 W. Second Street
Phone 644
Day and Night.

JOHN MILWARD CO.
Incorporated
Storage Warehouse.
Household Goods Moved,
Stored, Packed and
Shipped.
508-514 Maryland Avenue
Phone 644

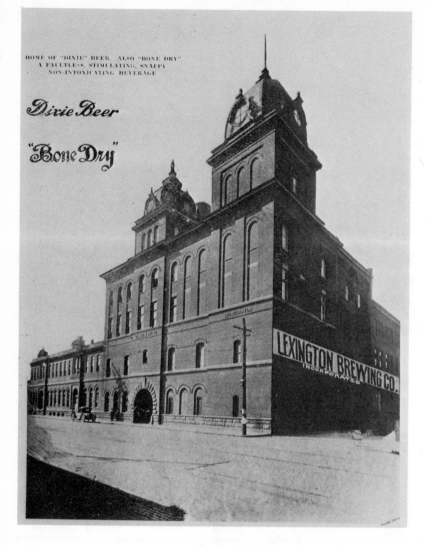

Lexington Brewing Company, Incorporated. John Gund, President; John Kloecker, Secretary.

Lexington Ice Company. Typical view of one of the rooms in the cold storage building.

Lexington Ice Company, exterior of Maxwell Ice Plant and Cold Storage Department.

This picture of the Lexington Ice Company, of the company delivery system, and view of Loudon Avenue Ice Storage Building was a panorama and had to be made into a one sided picture.

ELMENDORF COAL AND FEED CO.
Incorporated
WHOLESALE AND RETAIL
Coal, Grain, Hay, Feed Meal, and Building Material
Telephones 533 and 3164

Office, Yard and Elevator   Henry, Between Third and Fourth

DESCRIPTION

The new Lafayette Hotel illustrated herewith is to be the very latest creation of Hotel construction—viewed from the point of the home-loving class as well as the commercial public.

The design is Italian Rennaissance—12 stories high with well lighted basement—the base of building to be Pink Rockport Granite, and Buff Bedford Limestone—the shaft to be Tapestry Brick, soft shades of browns, purple and red, while the upper two stories are to be Matt glazed, Ivory white.

TERRA COTTA

The features of the plan are the large Lobby, which extends across the entire front of building, and which is to be 48 feet deep. The main entrance is on the axis of the Lobby, and directly in line with same—on the opposite side of Lobby is the Office. The West end of Lobby is to be elevated slightly to permit a view of the sunken gardens in front of the Depot. The East end of the Lobby is to be reserved for the Ladies. An attractive Ladies' entrance is to be provided, which leads directly to the Ladies Waiting and Retiring Room, and to the concourse leading to the Main Dining Room, which is to be located at the South-East corner of building.

There is a Marble stairway at each end of the Lobby to mezzanine—and the Telegraph — Telephone Rooms—Cigar and News Stands, and all the modern refinements of Hotel requirements have been nicely located.

The Lobby is designed to present an air of rest and comfort, and the decorations are to be carried out in keeping with this intention—the columns are to be paneled, and the walls wainscotted to a height of door opening with American Walnut, stained a Silver Grey.

The fireplace in alcove at end of Lobby and stairways are to be Tavernelle Marble, with the main walls above the wainscotting, an imitation stone of a lighter darker color than the marble.

The ceiling is beautifully beamed, paneled, and ornamented, and is to be an imitation of Caen Stone—the background is to be a dull gold, and the ornament and figures are to be picked out in blues, purples and reds—the color adding considerable interest.

L. B. SHOUSE, President

V. K. DODGE, Vice President

The floors, base and counters are to be a combination of Tennessee and Famosa Marble.

The Dining Room is to have walls of Caen stone, paneled between the pilasters with the panels decorated with mural decorations, a series of Italian garden scenes—at the end of Dining Room is to be an Orangerie, a pool and fountain—the ceiling to be beamed and paneled, and ornamented in low relief, which is to be picked out in color.

The Mezzanine floor is to comprise a lounging space around the entire Lobby—a handsome Ball and Banquet Room—Men's and Ladies' Retiring Rooms, private Dining Rooms, Writing and Reading Rooms.

The Ball Room is to be finished in two tones of Ivory white while the hangings and furniture coverings are to be a fine, figured velvet of mulberry color on an old gold background.

An attractive feature of the Mezzanine floor is the Loggia, overlooking the Garden in front of the Railroad Depot.

The Building will contain 300 guests rooms, each with a bath, and will comprise all the comforts of modern Hotel planning.

There will be a mechanical system of ventilation to change the air every ten minutes throughout all the principal rooms of building.

The basement will contain a Coffee Room—Barber Shop—Manicure and Billiard Rooms—Wash Rooms, etc., all mechanically ventilated.

There will be a complete refrigeration plant, running ice cold water in every room.

The building will have its own electric light plant, and lighting of building will be generous, with direct and indirect lighting fixtures.

The mechanical equipment will be the last word in engineering practice.

The Mason & Hanger Company are the contractors for the work; C. C. & E. A. Weber of Cincinnati are the Architects; Bert L. Baldwin of Cincinnati, is the Mechanical Engineer—and Lieberman Klein & Hein of Chicago are the Structural Engineers.

The Hotel as Contemplated will be one of the finest in the South, and a credit to the progressive life of Lexington.

SILAS B. MASON

LAFAYETTE HOTEL
Directors of Lafayette Hotel

L. B. Shouse, President
V. K. Dodge, Vice President
Silas B. Mason
Sam B. Walton
Louis Lee Haggin

Chas. R. Thompson
R. C. Estill
S. T. Harbison
John R. Downing
G. Nat. Pettit

Fred Stilz

**VICTOR BOGAERT
COMPANY**
Jewelers, Silversmiths,
Goldsmiths and Importers
Diamonds and Art Goods
Importing House
139 Chaussee de Waure,
Brussels, Belgium
American House Established
in Lexington, Kentucky
since 1883.

Interior view Victor Bogaert Company, Jewelers, Silversmiths, Goldsmiths and Importers.

NEW STORE OF JOHN A. KELLER CO.
(Incorporated)

FLORISTS

135 E. Main Street Opposite Phoenix Hotel   Phone 945

SAY IT WITH FLOWERS

Salesroom of L. A. Fennell, Florist, 151-15 N. Broadway, Phone 498.

Interior view of one of the Orchid Houses of L. A. Fennell taken before Xmas holidays.

Fitzgerald Plumbing & Heating Co. located at 132 South Limestone. They started in Maysville in 1893, moved to Lexington in 1903, and bought the Lexington Plumbing Co., which had been started in 1895. Fitzgerald later moved to Saunier Avenue.

J. M. Sullivan   H. G. Martin
M. J. Martin   G. B. Martin

SULLIVAN, MARTIN & CO.
Wholesale
Rough and Dressed Lumber
Office, Planing Mill and Yards
East Seventh St. and Hamilton Ave., on Belt Line
Lexington, Ky.

Mitchell, Baker & Smith
"Lexington's Quality Department Store"

Main Floor, Mitchell, Baker
& Smith's. "Lexington's
Quality Department Store."

United Clothing Stores for Men and Boys.   Next to Union Station, Lexington.

J. H. Hardesty Store sold various sundries, as you can see from the signs.

Opening day of Federal System Bakeries of Kentucky, corner Mill and Main Sts. June 7, 1919.

Feb 14, 1909.

UNION STATION, LEXINGTON, KY.

This picture of Union Station, Lexington was taken February 14, 1909. Later in time, flowers were planted in front.

This is one of the best views I have ever seen of the old Market House. Above Market House is where the Golden Gloves had their training center.

Chatham & Murray
Front of Sales Room

W. B. Stewart, Plumbing and
Heating, corner Church and
Mill, Phone 1538.

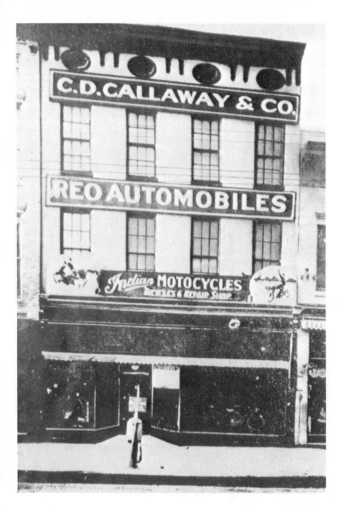

Callaway's Sporting Goods Store

REED HOTEL CO.
(Inc.)

J. H. Stillwell, President and General Manager   W. D. Sanders, Office Manager

No. 321-29 W. Short Street, One Block from Interurban

100 Rooms American or European Plan.   Popular Price

Commercial Auto Co., 245 East Main Street

Agents for Fayette County of Ford Cars and Parts. Keep on hand at all times the largest stock of Ford Parts of any Agent in Kentucky, their Shops for the repair of Ford cars are up to date and in charge of competent and courteous mechanics, who labor to please, and give satisfaction. Their line of Ford accessories, tires and tubes is very extensive, call and see them you will be assured of a Welcome, whether a customer or not. It is an unfortunate fact that the farmers of the South are the last to avail themselves of improved machinery for the advancement of agriculture. Silos were as common north of the Ohio as barns before the South began using them. It is the same way with the Farm Tractor, a tool that is as essential to an up-to-date farm, as a silo to a dairy. The Fordson Farm Tractor meets every requirement of the farm, as a plow tractor, as a seed tractor and as a stationary engine; they are essential to every farmer. We keep on hand these splendid machines, and also all parts for repair.

Be Up-To-Date — Get A Tractor

Lexington Cadillac Co.
Distributors for the
Cadillac in Central
Kentucky

Garage and Storage Department Lexington Cadillac Co.

Marshall-Featherston Motor Co. (Inc.)
Home of the Buick

Active Trading Scene
Kentucky Oil Exchange,
Lexington, Ky.

Warehouse of G. Z. Faulconer & Co.

Office and selling force of G. Z. Faulconer & Co.   First Row: 1. L. T. Rankin, 2. G. C. Douglas, 3. Geo. C. Roberts, Jr., 4. Earl Dickerson, 5. Geo. C. Roberts, Sr., 6. C. B. Calvert. Second Row: 7. W. T. Cox, 8, J. R. Sams, 9. G. Z. Faulconer, 10. Fred Boatwright, 11. A. M. Ridenour, Sr, 12. V. B. Faulconer. Third Row: 13. W. B. Jones, 14. G. F. Templeman, 15. A. M. Mounce, 16. W. C. Gritton, 17. W. C. Jones, 18. H. L. Tingle.

Laundry building and trucks. 1885, one colored man with basket, did the collecting and delivering. 1919, twelve trucks were used to make collections and deliveries.

Lexington Laundry Co. Officers and Directors, reading from left to right: Bottom Row — J. B. Mylor, Secretary; J. N. Williams, President and Treasurer; C. V. Powell, Vice President. Standing — C. S. Moore, A. C. Butler, W. L. Williams, D. V. Brown.

Office and Planing Mill — S. F. McCormick Lumber Co., Inc.

Section Lumber Yard — S. F. McCormick Lumber Co., Inc.

General View of Good Lumber
PERRY LUMBER CO.
"Everything In Lumber"
Building Contractors — Mill Work

Third Street and Walton Avenue   Phones: 512-3411

Office and Staff

Yard Entrance and Delivery Equipment

Section of yard showing our unloading facilities.

Some of those long leaf barn timbers you were thinking about.

Exterior Service Tire Co.

F. T. Justice & Co.
Coal, Lime, Sand and Cement

Office and Yard View

Concrete Sand and Rock Bins

Interior of Office

Side View Warehouse and Concrete Yard

Kentucky Motors Corporation

KENTUCKY MOTORS CORPORATION
Wm. B. Brown

High Grade Automobiles and Aeroplanes
"Honesty Is Our Policy"

420 West Main Street
Kentucky Motors Corporation

Office Kentucky Motors Corporation

Lexington's First and Only Aeroplane Agency

Lexington Roller Mills Co.

Incorporated

LEXINGTON, KY.

HENRY CLAY
FLOUR

—o—

THE PREMIER
FLOUR OF THE
SOUTH

LEXINGTON
CREAM FLOUR

—o—

KENTUCKY'S
BEST

THESE ARE THE BRANDS IN OUR BEST FLOUR
THEY ARE MORE ECONOMICAL—THEY TAKE LESS SHORTENING
"AINT IT THE TRUTH"

Plant of the Lexington Syrup and Beverage Co., 420-22-26-28 Christie St., Phone 1922.   Manufacturers of High Grade
Soft Drinks, Specialties — Club Soda and Lemon Sour, Distributors of Reif's Special.

Sales Room, Transylvania Printing Co., Office Outfitters and Stationers

Transylvania Printing Co.: Ruling Department, Composing Room, One of Our Cylinder Presses.

Combs Lumber Company, Main Office. Outside entrance 439 E. Main Street.

Combs Lumber Company, interior Main Office, 439 E. Main Street.

Combs Lumber Company, Yard, 439 E. Main Street

Waller Manufacturing Company, Incorporated. Furniture and Specialties, Anything Made from Lumber, West Main Street, Extended, Lexington, Kentucky. Special Cabinets, Cases, Lockers, Etc. Made to Order. Library Tables, Special Furniture, Tobacco Hogsheads, Tobacco Sticks, Boxes, Etc.

Woolcott Flour Mills, where Lexington Made Flour was Manufactured.

Lexington Wholesale Bakery Co.

Alex Hughes' Cash Grocery, East Second and Walnut Streets.

Roszell Bros. Wholesale and Retail Feed and Hay, Broadway and Boliver.

J. L. Rue & Son.   Staple and fancy groceries.   Main Street and Clay Avenue.

Downing Bakery Co.   "Lexington's Finest."   Oven and Sales Room.

McClure Photographic Supply Co.
Commercial Photographers

Plant of the Southern Bedding Co.
Mattress Manufacturers.

Filling Room

Stock Room

Finishing Room

Felting Room

W. R. Milward, Funeral Director, 159-163 N. Broadway.   Established 1867.   Office Phones 136, 336.
Motor equipment with private ambulance.   Residence phone 1989.

Office of W. R. Milward, Funeral Director

McAdams and Morford, Wholesale Druggists

Leland Hotel, Miss Mary Mooney, Prop.

Harp Bros., Lexington's Leading Grocers.   Established 1901.

Harp Bros., cleanest and most complete stock in Central Kentucky.

Becker Dry Cleaning Co.
Corner Limestone and High Street

Where clothes are steamed, pressed and sterilized.

Office

Dry Cleaning Room

Exterior Allen Electric Co.   Largest Contractors and Dealers South of the Ohio River.

Display Room Allen Electric Co.   Complete line of Electrical Supplies.

PLANING MILL OF HENDRICKS, MOORE & CO.
Incorporated

Phone 200-1027   Intersection of Georgetown & Newton

Office Force

Section of Lumber Yard
Where barns are framed for erection.

PLANT OF W. I. PETTY CO.

Stemming Room No. 1

Stemming Room No. 2

This was the Main Street Christian Church after its purchase by contractors in 1892. Barnum and Bailey Circus was coming to town on October Eighth. Dr. Pierce's Golden Medical Discovery for blood, liver, and lungs and Bull Durham Tobacco for 5 cents were advertised.

Broadway Christian Church, Broadway and Second Streets, Lexington, Kentucky. Dedicated May 4, 1919. The congregation worshipping in this building was organized in 1870. The building recently dedicated was the third building occupied by this congregation.

Administration Building,
University of Kentucky

Residence of Dr. F. L. McVey
President, University of Kentucky

Patterson Hall

Gymnasium

FAUX PAS

***

Page VII	Acknowledging my thanks to the Charles Staples family in respect to the late Charles Staples.
Page 22 (below)	Miss Lucy G (not Lucky) Shelby. With them lived (not lives) their nephew.
Page 26 (below)	Mammouth (not Mammouths) Garage.
Page 29 (above)	Home of Dr. J. G. Foster was (not is) located.
Page 29 (below)	Higgins' home was (not is) located behind Maxwell Presbyterian Church (not East High) near Lexington Ave.
Page 31 (below)	"The Meadows" was located on East Loudon Avenue.
Page 35 (below)	The Geohagans home was situated on W. High St.
Page 38 (below)	Dr. Dudleys' residence and office was situated on the old Paris Road.
Page 42 (below)	Betty Powell Rodes (not Roades) Joe Logan Massie (not Joe Logan).
Page 43 (below)	Mr. Gunn (not Dunn) was listed.
Page 46 (above)	The building to the right (not left) later became the University Book Store owned by Frank Battaile.
Page 46 (below)	Showing the site where the Fayette National Bank and later the First Security National Bank & Trust was built.
Page 52 (below)	were (not was) taken from the saloon walls.
Page 72 Asterisk	Pittsburgh Phil and Riley (not Ronnie) Grannon.
Page 76	Catholic (not small c) Church.

Sincere apologies (pour une autre perrson)

Barton K. Battaile